The Undertow

University of Central Florida Contemporary Poetry Series

UNIVERSITY PRESS OF FLORIDA

Gainesville · Tallahassee · Tampa · Boca Raton
Pensacola · Orlando · Miami · Jacksonville

Susan Snively

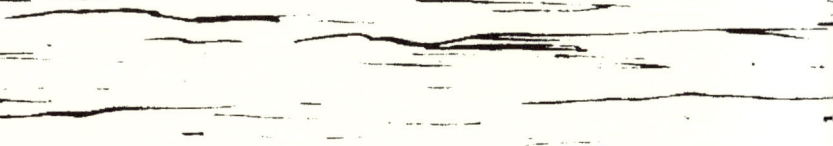

The Undertow

Also by Susan Snively:
From This Distance (1981)
Voices in the House (1988)

Copyright 1997 by the Board of Regents of the State of Florida
Printed in the United States of America on acid-free paper
All rights reserved

03 02 01 00 99 98 c 6 5 4 3 2 1
03 02 01 00 99 98 p 6 5 4 3 2 1

LIBRARY OF CONGRESS CATALOGING-IN-PUBLICATION DATA
Snively, Susan, 1945–
The undertow / Susan Snively.
p. cm. — (Contemporary poetry series / University of Central Florida)
ISBN 0-8130-1568-5 (acid-free paper). —
ISBN 0-8130-1569-3 (pbk.: acid-free paper)
I. Title. II. Series: Contemporary poetry series (Orlando, Fla.)
PS3569.N5U53 1998
811'.54—dc21   97-29747

The University Press of Florida is the scholarly publishing agency for the State University System of Florida, comprised of Florida A & M University, Florida Atlantic University, Florida International University, Florida State University, University of Central Florida, University of Florida, University of North Florida, University of South Florida, and University of West Florida.

University Press of Florida
15 Northwest 15th Street
Gainesville, FL 32611
http://nervm.nerdc.ufl.edu/~upf

in memory of my parents

Wie er auf
dem letzten Hügel, der ihm ganz sein Tal
noch einmal zeigt, sich wendet, anhält, weilt,—
so leben wir und nehmen immer Abschied.

Rainer Maria Rilke, "Duino Elegy VIII"

Contents

Acknowledgments xi

TRAVELERS 1

At the Fish Lift 3
Surf Caster 5
Spencer Tracy 6
Airports 7
The Auld Sod 9
Roast Chicken 11
The Balloon 13
Too Late 14
Afterwords 16
A Boat of Widows 17
Travelers 20

THE SPEED OF THE DRIFT 21

Notes 36

ANOTHER LIFE 37

Siberians 39
Talk to the Wall 40
White Twilight 42
Shepherd on the Rocks, with a Twist 43
A Woman Holding a Balance 47
Jane Austen in January 48
The Death of the Fall 49
The Shape 50

Algebra 51
Second Glance 52
Distance 53
Another Life 54

THE UNDERTOW 57

Acknowledgments

"The Balloon" and sections VI, VIII, and IX of "The Speed of the Drift" appeared in *The Massachusetts Review* (Spring 1989, Summer 1992).

"Algebra" and sections VII and XVIII of "The Speed of the Drift" appeared in *Shenandoah* (Fall 1991, Fall 1993).

Sections I, II, VII, XXIII, and XXV of "The Speed of the Drift" were privately printed in *The Speed of the Drift: An Excerpt* by the ELM Press (Wallingford, Penn., 1992).

"The Shape," "A Woman Holding a Balance" (both Fall 1989), and "Talk to the Wall" (Spring 1995) appeared in *Poetry East*.

"Another Life" appeared in *Ploughshares* (Winter 1993–94).

"The Death of the Fall" appeared in *Smith Voices: An Anthology of Smith Writers*, ed. Patricia Skarda (Northampton, Mass.: Smith College, 1990).

"At the Fish Lift," in an earlier form, won Honorable Mention in the Gertrude Claytor Poetry Award competition of the Poetry Society of America, 1993.

Travelers

At the Fish Lift
Holyoke, Mass.

Into the elevator, tumbled by the rush
of sulfur-colored water,
shad, bass, and herring pour
to be hauled above the dam
into the next lap of the long swim
toward the destined spawning,
the pure aerobic leap in early evening.

At the viewing-tank
we watch their sinuous traffic,
wide-eyed with purpose or confusion,
some apparently talking,
a few veterans bearing fuchsia bruises,
shad mammas heavy with roe,
tiny stripers, eely lamprey
with wide sucking lips,
primordial sturgeon, whose bottom fins
look like wanna-be feet,
and the odd salmon that brings forth a shout
from a big-booted worker with a net.

The power plant, a welfare state
in cacophonous microcosm,
is clean and full of facts,
earnest, ungrammatical signs,
maps of the mothers and daughters of rivers,
old photos of Irish and French-Canadians
heaving shad-filled buckets.

We are all mostly water,
so we let it claim us,
the lone noun, *fish,* alive in the mouth
like a tongue.

Fresh wind hassles the trees below the dam;
black-backed gulls and cormorants
make an inland party: easy fast food,
their own latrine on a retaining wall,
a tolerant crowd.

The sign in the shining entryway
near the blasted, pocked parking lot
says every fish counts
and someone counts them,
proof that the river
is cleaning up an old bad act
with nothing more than the usual twists
and turns. Unconscious, single-minded,
the fish join the newly redeemed
among the numberless,
held for a time in the almighty scales.

Surf Caster

Again and again you cast into the sea.
I watch your eyes, intent under wild brows,
the careful swing of your arms. Nothing,
again nothing. The blue I saw
was a phantom? You say no,
fish have their own laws,
like the grammar of a cloudy language,
and try as we might we'll never know it.
So I have to learn
not to be sorry for an empty line,
its three teeth clean and bloodless,
a morning spent to no purpose
but beholding the habits of the random,
or better, getting used to seeing you
do what you love best (or second best),
your body and mind tuned to lifts and drops,
the long wait for a grateful rapture.

Spencer Tracy
Key West

In the rinsed bubble of Sunday morning,
the plastic roosters on the sarcophagi
are rescued from melting
by a January breeze flavored with north.
Cobalt-blue and lime-green beads
shimmer in Elizabeth Bishop's doorway,
the colors brightening minute by minute.
Later, when the clouds have moved to Cuba,
Hemingway's cats come out to be fed—
Marilyn Monroe, blonde, sumptuous, toothless;
mean, grizzled Spencer Tracy; Jennifer Jones,
a wayward opportunist; and Gertrude Stein,
who is just as I imagined,
solid, repetitive, a picky feeder.
Here is the afterlife, or its beginnings,
the first stage of the last question
"Where am I?"
answered only by the next meal, a diversion,
a boat clearing the horizon
all at once. It will take time to unload
its suspicious cargo. Spencer Tracy, in his Hyde-suit,
shows Jennifer his teeth. He's old and put-upon.
There's a lot about the world he doesn't like
but he claims it anyway,
his property, littered with felled fruit.

Airports

Much have I traveled in the realms of Delta,
BOAC, Icelandic. In airport lounges,
tuned to my number like a show-dog,
I always hope to meet a familiar face.
I've never met Walter Cronkite, but my mother
danced with him once at a journalists' convention.
Fabulous dancer, she said. "Oh, you're the one,"
he would not say to me, "I danced with your mother
in '68." I wouldn't dare to tell him
about my early worship of newsmen,
their ironies, bad jokes, dirty fingers,
or my faith in the facts he spelled on "You Are There"
in punchy trochaic Midwestern.

It'd be pleasant to run into Bunny Nelson,
a girl I knew in school, popular, pretty,
not particularly a friend of mine.
I can see her now: freckled, her dark-blonde hair
a reliable taupe, her good teeth still even;
probably married to a lawyer, or a lawyer
herself, or head of a school committee.
I remember the long slow way she said "orange,"
followed by the flip of a giggle. Surprise,
wary politeness, a look at my roots,
then a rapid valedictory catalogue—
Tammy dried-out, Boo vanished, Lee divorced.
Maybe we've read the same book recently.
Possession by A.S. Byatt's the one I'd hope for.

You can tell a great deal about a person
by how she reacts to a big juicy novel.

And since time is fleeting, even in airplanes
where midnight and dawn are mirror-images,
I wouldn't mind (I guess I wouldn't mind)
spending a couple of hours with my first husband,
as long as he's not accompanied by his mother.
He'd talk a lot, mostly complain
in perfectly diagrammable sentences
like the Blake notes he took in grad school.
Being forbidden to smoke would spark his humor,
the animal-metaphors, the victim-mishaps,
the books he never got around to reading
and the many he did I wouldn't read for money.

Usually I see the same bland
aggregate of souls, of which I am one,
none of us famous or familiar, and only
worth a story if we arrive in bags.
No nuns this trip. Or they're in disguise,
like writers. Nuns don't look like nuns anymore,
and writers look like everyone, only more worn,
older for staring into pitiless light.

The Auld Sod

All of my Scottish ancestors are dirt
and they were dirty long before they died.
Their favorite proverb said, "Mair dirt, less hurt,"
a natural source of toughness in the hide.

They thought a hut was cozier when "clarty,"
and milk more flavorful when churned by frogs
(and even tastier when frogs were warty).
They mixed their butter with the hairs of dogs.

Soap was unknown: it hadn't been invented.
Two baths a lifetime were, it seems, enough.
Unlike the French, the Scottish were contented
without the flattery of the powder-puff.

Unappetizing ignorance, or sin
externalized, a masochistic dip
in dirt for dirt's sake, that adorns the skin
with flowers of filth? That Presbyterian drip

John Knox, when set upon by lice and fleas,
secretly bid his inwit to invite
bold images to torment him and tease
that he might suffer folks to walk upright.

His contribution to the Reformation,
with all its watchfulness and grim intent,
helped to ensure the rigorous conflation
of venality with excrement.

There is a logic here I understand.
I traffic in its meanness when I dream
acts of revenge unprinted by my hand,
a hand as purely white as clotted cream.

The tubers skirling in a pot of water
require high temperatures to make them food,
as clannish habits of attack and slaughter
demand a battle cry to steam the blood.

All in good time, a fierceness in the haunches
succeeds to stories told around a fire;
the little ones held closely, see the branches
consumed in glory as the coals expire,

and wonder at their hunger, unappeased
but peaceful in the fantasizing dusk
that seizes words like animals, both eased
and mad to gnaw the meat and spit the husk.

"Dour" is the word for them, my ancient kin.
It's not the word for me, but deep inside,
beneath the tenderized and prickly skin,
I know their hunger and their stupid pride.

They know—because they're barely civilized
and yet as civilized as people come
who live in hovels, undeodorized
by bourgeois Cleaning-Lady-in-a-Drum—

the swine that rootles in the muddy pen,
the sheep dumbly agape under the knife,
will sacrifice their hides to language when
they cease to be necessities of life.

I wouldn't want them cleaner than they are.
They have been cleansed of centuries of grime
and stink no more, their history a star
shining as best it can, through wastes of time.

Roast Chicken

I'd like to make a roast chicken again
for my first husband. It was the first thing
I ever learned to cook. Julia said
you couldn't be a cook unless you learned
to turn out a chicken, golden-amber, moist,
basted with butter every fifteen minutes.
I'd hover over it, tender and maternal,
listening for the rain of little splutters
announcing the final crisping of the skin.
My roast chicken was as close as we came
to being parents, grateful for the bird's
perfect health, its willingness to accept
compliments, to give broth from its bones.
Whatever was wrong became a bit less wrong
when the trouble I took became a ceremony.
A roast chicken was our child, our church.

And poor old R., my demon lover, now dead,
would have lived a longer, healthier life
if he'd been willing to eat my food with gusto
and not submit to the martyrdom of his ulcers.
I couldn't have fixed his craziness or violence
by filling his plate with pale rosy breast meat,
but maybe—if a meal can offer a home
for wayward senses weary of self-harassment—
he could have seen his cursed life as a blessing,
as a stove is more a campfire than the grill
on which St. Lawrence reached his hard perfection.

As for my former stepchildren and their father,
well, I would cook a chicken even for them,
if only to retrieve the far-flung moments
of beatitude around the dinner table.
It's hard to dislike those for whom you cook,
whose teeth chew the food you bought and fixed,
whatever else their mouths may do or say
after the dishes are cleared and the evening stretches
its tired limbs beside the mercurial firelight.

The hardest thing about my parents' deaths
is that I'll never cook for them again,
never make up for years of picky refusals,
indifference, or ignorance of what
it took to put a dinner on the table.
But it isn't expiation or regret
for sin I'm feeling, rather something simpler,
like looking every morning for the sun,
knowing it is there but utterly hidden,
and likely to stay that way for a long time.

I bend over the body, brush in hand,
and smell the tarragon and lemon peel
crisping in the cavity. Never mind
that it is female, splayed upon its back,
legs tied up, submissive, robbed of its guts,
headless, its inner thoughts unimaginable.
So what if it's me in another form, so what
if its skin has turned the color of my hair,
and parts of me are made from what it was?
This is as close to happiness as I come.
The heated blood is blossoming in my face.

The Balloon

As its tail sashays up to heaven
above still houses and kids in yards,
we all fall silent, the little ones
busy digging the roots' intricate clay;
the parents, kind, instructive
over bikes and wagons,
until one by one, fingers
point, eyes on the tips
curl shut, defeated
by so much space released into a day.

Under the slab rock
my father has laid Caesar the cat. The dogs,
the foxes, no one will find him out,
taking his own time with his afterlife,
a prospect I'll secretly fathom with him
when the need comes. It makes sense,
this spaciousness trailing off into *nothing,*
the word drying on my lips,
replaced, the longer I look
at my heart flying away from me everywhere,
by *everything* becoming more vast
as it takes us up, and in.

Too Late

It's too late to become a ballet dancer.
At nine, I could execute piqué turns
like a dervish, faster than the other girls.
My arms were supple as grass. But now
I get a little dizzy, trying a turn
or three in the kitchen when nobody's home.
Look what happened to poor Zelda Fitzgerald,
practicing arabesques to a scratchy record
of "Valencia." It only goes to show—
if age doesn't get you, bad taste will.

It's too late to become a famous actress.
I teach, therefore I act, especially reading
poetry aloud, hoping to move
someone to tears or fright, or to stop
their chewing gum and staring out the window.
But always I feel I may have gone too far.
A student praised me once, on a course survey,
"Ms. S. can do so many interesting accents."

It's not likely I'll be a nuclear physicist,
although I was once overjoyed to learn
how small the nucleus is, hanging inside
its atom like a dust mote in a basilica.
I realize now that what I know of physics
is like a dust mote inside the whole round world,
and that what fascinated me at twelve
was disaster, always just about to happen.

My awe was a useful substitute for religion,
but not, alas, the real thing. Nor will I

become a singer, although I have sung
and occasionally receive a compliment
from someone who doesn't know much about singing.
High D is gone, taking high C with her,
and good old B-flat isn't what she should be.
Now and then, singing along with a tape,
I'll note a curious wobble, like cooked spaghetti,
underneath my usually bang-on pitch.
Oh, it's the car, the bumpy road, I'll think,
but no, it's something else. Neglect. Age.

There's still time to be a decent cook,
a glutton jeweled with the glaze of manners,
eager to please while pleasuring her mouth.
I used to say I'd rather write than eat,
but now I'm not so sure. To love a word,
wine, for example, is to love the thing
itself, as well as the occasion—
voluptuous evening hour, sybarite friends—
that stirs it into shimmer, so that reflection
tastes the same as a life without regret.

Afterwords

Imagine the first words invented
were not *danger, food, run,*
but *guilty, cute, dysfunctional,*
vagrants that cruise the language
to scope its chancy byways,
bored, waiting for a buzz.

How could we have survived
without them? That's a *cute*
saber-toothed tiger; Dad feels *guilty*
after the big feast; my bones are
dysfunctional when it rains.
Inside the well-appointed house,
late in this self-conscious century
laboring its big lies,
I sit at the dining table
with my head in my hands. The food
has turned cold, the hair sharpens
on the back of my head. My despair
is cute, which used to mean pointed,
accurate, as in another 'cute remark
thrills—which used to mean trembles—
in the vertebrae. Danger burns the air
like thunder, for which there are still no words,
only hiding until it runs by,
or standing at the window,
silently calling it to come.

A Boat of Widows

At Arsenale, the vaporetto waits.
They step aboard, carrying bouquets
of sumptuous spring lilies. Their good coats
are various shades of cinnamon. Their days,
it would appear, are spent in taking care
of what is left: hands and face and hair
by which they know the knowing world can tell
whether in marriage they were treated well.

Care of appearances becomes in time
an art beyond self-conscious decoration,
as *taste* marries in its full-blown rhyme
the *taste* that starts as love of pure sensation.
I watch a child reach toward the swaying buds,
his face imperially handsome. Heads
turn; a hand wearing a ring of pearls
confirms the springing tendril of his curls.

Gazing at strangers, I can only guess
at destiny, the deep anonymous life
that women of old countries wear in dress
and jewelry, as if the names of wife,
widow, or lover, are at once disguise
and revelation. Art that beautifies
has always helped appease the question, why
bother with the body that must die?

On San Michele, coming into view,
the gothic cypress spires, sharply black,

soften as we approach the dock. A few
pilgrims await the boat to take them back.
I am aware of how I read the scene
in emblematic, neo-Puritan
schemas of the overbearing word
that even Virgil might have found absurd.

The widows gather briefly, then unravel
in the vast garden, empty of all sound
except the songs of birds and crunch of gravel.
We've come to find the newly opened ground
of Brodsky's grave, but learn he still awaits
transport and fancy papers from the States.
The dead are covered in punctilio,
he might have said. The living let them go

only after long successive drafts
of speeches have reduced them, shade by shade,
to early tremulous inklings of their gifts,
before the weighty prize and accolade.
Grief is a lightening, although it takes
the time it needs after the time it takes,
and after that, memorial acts ensue—
as on Diaghilev's grave, a ballet shoe

mildews in rain but keeps its perfect curve
instructed by a foot that used to leap,
perhaps one of the widows' now, who move
through their unfettered days from sleep to sleep,
or just an ordinary dancer who
found in good time what gravity will do
to aerial flesh, and thought it wise to make
this gesture for kinetic memory's sake.

Ferried back among a talky crowd
of backpacked kids, I look around for widows,
but they have vanished into sea or cloud
or their lives' unknowable lights and shadows,

a tribute to La Serenissima's
power to take up loss and let it pass
into deep waters, leaving in its place
changeable smiles on my distracted face.

Travelers

Imagine you have surrendered your fare
and taken your hard seat. The boatman
turns his back and lifts up the oars,
still tireless despite the daily labor
that will last, he knows, forever.
You settle back—or rather, since your bones
have lightened their burden—
you become as one with the boat
as it moves forward into darkness.
After a while you could say to your neighbor,
"Isn't it taking awfully long?"
But he wouldn't be able to answer,
never having made this journey,
and in fact you never ask the question,
since time is the memory of a bright stream
watched from the lip of a cliff,
its tumbles and rushes a serene silence.
Fog moves its skirts aside, drops flags,
shreds spill away from shreds,
and gray is a hundred colors.
How peaceful it is. The crying baby sleeps now
in its grandmother's arms. The injured citizens
lift up their heads. You can hear them
breathing, listening to their freedom.
Wasn't life always like this
in each of its passing moments
before you stepped into knowledge
to be carried away?

... *You know, they straightened out the Mississippi River in places, to make room for houses and livable acreage. Occasionally the river floods these places. "Floods" is the word they use, but in fact it is not flooding, it is remembering. Remembering where it used to be. All water has a perfect memory and is forever trying to get back to where it was.*

Toni Morrison,
"The Site of Memory"

The Speed of the Drift

The Speed of the Drift

I

Water crept up, lapping. I watched it
heave its salty weeds above the brown stones,

until at sharp noon, an hour later
than yesterday's dank, inconsequential tide,

the sea entered the pink granite fissure,
laboring to keep its appointment.

The rocks broke open my thoughts.
Water drifts, forgets, remembers, and is not sad

as the tides of the body are sad, falling away
or relieved from the pursuit of fullness.

But why think of this at all?
Is the mind a moon, passively predestined,

stirred by the reflex a casual will makes?
Language stood on the edge, a transparent companion.

It came to me because I am a human
and a mind is the one thing we cannot help.

II

June 24. A Sunday, sun bursting open the flowers.
The irises' dried fists give way to cosmos,

lamb's ears, foxglove—names she would have loved,
fresh from an old, inventive, humorous world.

The ground's a bed of miracles.
After some delicious play in the dirt

I pack up the kitchen. It is terminal,
ready for gutting. The diagnostic word

stops my hands. This is the day—
a day like this, golden-pink, she died

quieted and swollen, at home in bed
attended by privileged friends, years ago.

Her death was no good thing. Whatever good
may come of it lies only in the light,

making its way through the still-breathing forest,
that reaches me from where she was,

where she is, in some deep-rooted work
that keeps me busy and mystified.

III

When he walked down the street, the color yellow
followed him, barking, begging for candy.

He turned his face. The scenery fell apart
the way the face of his wife would crumple

when he took it in his hands.
He loved the dark places where he could hide words

not from lies or echoes,
but from the noisy eggs

hatching in his brain. Even the word *thing*
carried around a dense head of steam.

He fought the smoke, trying to forget.
The doctor said there was more to a man

than a manic memory, but outside it
he was a skinless dwarf, a temporary guest

in the world. "I never understood," he said,
"that time could move on without me.

Watching the colors of the handkerchiefs,
I did not even try to catch the train."

IV

The little boy sings the song they make him sing.
When the grown man sings the song, his voice

is almost a child's, his face a pleasant mask.
His eyes look past the camera into history,

where explanations for the crimes he witnessed
fall like sickly, desiccated seeds.

Of the six million, I think he is
the six million and first, a living guest

beyond grief or love. He stands in the field,
pointing, mechanical as a dummy by the road

with its tireless Nazi-salute.
The smiles of terrible villagers surround him,

fishhooks dangling into a well,
but he has already been caught and cleaned.

His face is unbearable to look at,
the face of a man who has lost his place in time,

who says, if a wet cheek is pressed to his dry one,
"Thank you, please, thank you again, thank you."

V

"Forsake me not thus, Adam." The piteous words
look different when I underline *thus,*

making Eve smarter than she seemed:
"If you're going to leave, don't go off half-cocked."

The blind poet, stepping out on a blue-white road,
must have heard the rustling behind him

as of a gown dropping slowly to her knees.
Helplessness would follow on command.

A patchy mist lay all before him,
hiding the future he needed to beget.

Meanwhile, Eve had no way to know
there were other men in the world

less moody, defensive, etc. (words concealed
under the hard carapace of marriage).

She felt her naked arms. The silk gown
was, she saw, just a pile of leaves.

She was a child, really, and always would be,
but for humanity's sake she had to fake it.

VI

We closed eyes, then bowed heads for the crash.
Chattering in the brown fog, the plane

smacked into landing. Laughter, applause.
I walked toward my friend across wavery tarmac,

hoping to tell the story in comfort,
but when light fell into a hole in his face,

I saw how the new pills had not cured him.
The slow exposure of these memories

says every event has a ghost-event
where the best and worst that could have happened

are, as Blake says, an image of the truth.
The nervous tale-spinner, wary of free-floating wreckage,

suppresses the pictures. But there they are,
the ecstatic couple, running toward each other.

The blue and white stripes on her dress
flow into an oblivious backwash. How could they know

that soon their bodies would turn into minds,
their loss become whatever they chose to lose?

VII

If I touched his hand
some harm would flow as from a fatal drink.

The moment struggled to lift itself free.
A cold wave coursed through a warm wave,

scattered the radio noise of conversation,
eased back the open blades of the lips.

Late fall, trees held bronze cargoes,
a scrim over the visible world

suspended the actual green behind sepia.
The past tense went on with its business.

A mere breath (I could hear it gathering) would wreck
the fullness, as a hidden director

parted the fabric and clapped his hands.
I withdrew my hand from the charged space

and resumed the plain cloak of speech,
trailing a few scuffed leaves.

VIII

I promised to be with him when he died.
Death was a small gray cloud

parked over Lake Baikal or Sumatra,
far from a room where flower-smells

drifted into the happy sound of a mower.
The morning took all morning and all afternoon

to complete itself and dress in evening clothes.
I didn't forget what we said. I haven't

forgotten the promises I've broken
along with the vows. But it seems,

reading the intensifying weather,
spelling with my fingers

between the lines of a half-completed letter,
it seems I will not be there for him.

I could hope he would have forgotten the promise,
forgotten the morning it was made,

when his body, easing into its long-practiced act,
told him he would probably live forever.

IX

Beyond us—but do we really believe that?
Don't the dying simply want a little rest,

having not settled the question?
Every self-portrait is an inquiry,

even Dürer's, with his long athletic neck,
his chain-mail hair and skeptical glance.

Rembrandt's wrinkles, the punctuation of doubt,
hide some residual, wry self-love.

Those countless heads of state pressed upon money
proclaim, "I am the total coin you spend;

years from now, I can save you from the bread-line."
Dürer didn't know he'd come to look like Bob Dylan,

arrogant, tuneless, with all the right words
for those who thought wisdom was memorization.

We thought nothing was beyond us in those days,
sitting around a loft, trading echoes,

afraid to look deeply in the mirror
past the hair, the wild colors, and the smoke.

X

We invented the Seven Deadlies to keep from knowing
dozens of more unnameable sins

bred in the dank memorious crevices
between bloated pity and self-love's proud flesh.

The old sinner thinks, chews on a pen,
then inscribes the event's red insides

delicately, to save his life
hidden in his own, sheepish in his wolf-suit.

The blood that flowed onto the sheets
has dried into a stain the color of bourbon.

With all his limbs and letters intact
he sentences himself, but the words' momentum

propels him toward a meeting
he has arranged in a large hotel,

a table reserved discreetly behind palms.
"Lust?" he would say, greeting his companion.

"Avarice," she replies, with sibilant niceness.
They bow their heads over the all-consuming menu.

XI

The old black hickory bears a scar
of raddled violence. Hugging the house,

it cannot know its saving grace, the lightning-stroke
like white hair on the head of the fleeing prisoner

running too fast to feel heat from the bullet.
In the morning sun the tree steams quietly,

hours of breath without the help of lungs.
For the hickory, *to do* is simply *to be,*

all its experience—which we call memory
even when forgotten—seared and gnawn

into the skin. Simply to bear
means to carry, to suffer, to lose, to perpetuate,

so many acts all at once, strung out
through the years, with no knowledge,

even the sudden fall of its gift and burden,
clear yellows lightening the ground.

XII *(for Will Parker)*

He sang, not with the memory of a voice
but with the real thing, in spite of his wasted body,

his gaunt face, his neck stained with sarcoma.
Listening, we remember and forget,

wrapped in skirling resonance.
The words I wrote for him, that never were mine

but simply started here, have now condensed
into a planet of music. The razor's edge

where he stands, held against the hip of the piano,
lights up like a runway for Mercury

hurling message after message into the crowd
from his chamber of turbulence.

For a moment, losing touch with gravity,
I imagine he could go on singing

in the labor that is his joy and will,
a fury that recomposes time.

XIII *(for Tomas Tranströmer)*

The poetry that holds us is water
where some of us are fish, others rice-grains,

or floating molecules of matter
waiting for an electrical charge.

The face of the poet is the North Sea
humbled by calm. From the thick life below,

fine glassy strands drift to the surface.
He has learned that a voice is a small thing

except when he uses it as he can,
calling to us through the twisted tunnels,

or on miracle nights, surfacing together
to fill our lungs with populous air.

In the night sky, an accidental blessing,
Venus dangling from the moon's sickle,

makes us believe in an intricate magic,
something to trade in secret with each other,

that the poet would honor above speech itself,
a spark played from stone to stone.

XIV

Turn away from the story, turn back,
and in a few days it looks different

as the small white lights on the town trees
wink with jolly hypocrisy or craven hope

into the gaudy fronts of the stores
anxious to be disembarrassed.

It is so hard to say
that you tried to love and failed,

or rather that your failure joined to another's
as the bittersweet tangles with the winterberry

near the hopeful bulbs of the crocus.
The darting arrows of projection

fly about like pointed hail.
Under the ground of memory

the forces of rot and blossom
eat at the same roots.

XV

The secret was to make cruelty look so busy
the eye darted everywhere at once,

forgetting that no blood on the trampled snow
meant blood waited to spill behind the scenes.

They knew as well the dirty secret of living:
that children, being innocent, would take

food from any stranger and sleep anywhere,
gnawing a bone of sugar soaked in gin.

Later someone paints over the picture,
making the children chickens and sacks of grain;

their screams, like all historical cries,
are muffled by newsprint, while a crafty demagogue

works another crowd in the same square.
All but a few—sad-eyed,

with scarred backs—turn their faces upwards,
hoping, as always, for a little good news.

XVI

Trying to play chess, the wounded Russian soldiers
push kings and queens into the dark red squares,

their brains' gutted suburbs.
The bishop, sharpest to a half-blind touch,

his offer of salvation reduced in scale,
seems to mock his own substance as mere relic.

Hunched over the board, cradling headaches,
the men dart their hands forward, snatch them back,

frostbitten among imaginary fires.
The youngest one gives up, opens his diary,

shuts his eyes, tells his hand to write,
a scout that sneaks past his tricky, unstrung eyes.

Each misspelled word looks like a bloody footprint.
"I have to be the one to tell you. War must end.

This is the only password left to me
since I lost the body of my knowledge."

XVII

When the bearded doctor asks Jimmie
"Seen me before?" Jimmie says, "No, doc,

think I'd ever forget a beard like that?"
—the same reply for fourteen years.

In his mind he's nineteen, it's September, 1945,
the first of many lucky days held in the pack,

although his raw face grays in the mirror.
His wires to the present, unstrung by booze,

are a tissue of blitzed connections. Aren't we lucky,
every day adding jokes and stories

to the buffer, taking our friends by surprise,
ha-ha, but never taken aback

by the new drugs, forms of weaponry or speed
the busy world gets up to? Where was our past

when we needed it? Over and done for,
its drying face a riddle in the glass.

XVIII

Long grasses in the stream waver, subside,
ride up, a continual harassment.

Lithe as a dendrite, the current
carries a message from the brains of earth

into the forgetful motions of air.
Blake saw nature as a myth of separation,

parent rended from child, flesh from thought,
partings still shuddering from the fall

felt by everything alive.
Silent, the orphans gather around,

reeds move as one in the deepening shade.
The careless passing of molecules

disguised as water might have been,
with a mere flicker of an atmosphere,

disintegrating earth or yearning grass,
or the long farewell that feels like a sheet of fire.

XIX

Poised, lonely on his turtleback rock,
the herring gull I watched grow up

from white-brown to gray-white,
raucous and hungry to well-fed,

guards his post. His search for a mate
commands his whole will, if will is what he has,

the pulse of pure consciousness, timed
to the speed of the drift that brings in fish,

takes fish away. He's a handsome creature.
I wish him luck, since I know

that in the fog-blind, character's no gift.
I fold up in the quiet, a piece of paper

someone has changed into a small white bird,
whose language, unanswered by the tide,

has become a familiar, overworked puzzle.
No harm. The fog opens a beam, no, a thread

of sun, like the fishing line of a friend
far down the coast, beckoning these waters.

Notes

II. The poet Sarah Youngblood, 1929–1980.

III. A. R. Luria's *The Mind of a Mnemonist* (1968) describes the remarkable memory of his patient "S," who used synaesthetic connections to retain passages of words or numbers. Of "S," Luria writes, ". . . one would be hard put to say which was more real for him: the world of imagination in which he lived, or the world of reality in which he was but a temporary guest."

IV. Simon Srebnik in Claude Lanzmann's film *Shoah*. As a child, Srebnik worked at the concentration camp at Chelmno, where he saved his life by singing a sentimental Polish song for the guards.

V. *Paradise Lost,* Book IX.

XV. Brueghel, *The Massacre of the Innocents.* The Hampton Court version of the painting shows the massacred children as sacks of grain and fowl.

XVI. A. R. Luria's *The Man with the Shattered World* (1972) tells the history of a soldier, Zarsetsky, wounded near Smolensk in World War II. Zarsetsky's wound left him unable to read or to remember anything he had learned, but through great effort he managed to write a history of his illness.

XVII. Oliver Sacks, in *The Man Who Mistook His Wife for a Hat* (1985), describes Jimmie, "the lost mariner," victim of Korsakoff's syndrome, which destroyed his short-term memory and left him permanently confused about time.

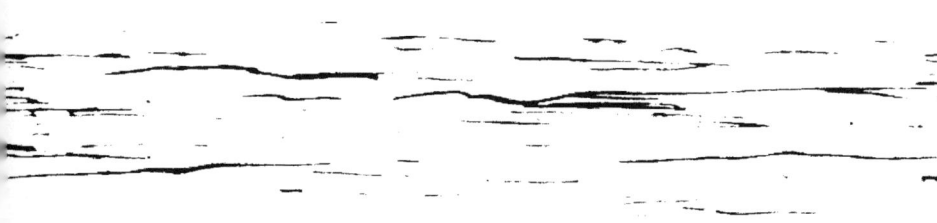

Another Life

Siberians

Little White, Summer Skies, Dreaming Spires—
unearthly purple-blue
floating over the swamp-haze—
I have their names by heart.

To remember too much,
not just the times when failed love
ceased, for awhile, to fail,
but the unexpected lights and shades
of neighborhoods long abandoned,
leafy wings, sweet-and-sour bluegrass,
all I have to do is look
through the half-open door
at dinnertime, wooden spoon in hand,
trying to hide in the sight.

A little purposeful movement
to a stove and back, arranging
my husband's plate with fresh greens and yellows
for one of the last times,
does not restore the spirit.
There's too much blue out there,
and white so pure it makes a light of its own,
touched softly with gold, like candles cupped
against the sinister fresh wind.

Talk to the Wall

A fox sped through the grass,
over the buried horse-bones, so quickly
I could believe that only my eyes caught him,

that only I knew his promise
of danger and escape. Fireflies rose and fell
over the wall of a newspaper.

Behind it, the wall of a mind intent on itself.
Spring peepers were trying out
their metallic nocturnes, sex in the air

if nowhere else. I stayed put,
inhaling the smoke from the grill
where I made nightly miracles

without the hope of saints. On the surface
of the landscape about to be changed,
I dug and planted primary colors.

Like neutral ground that is our only good,
or an animal that warms under a slow stare,
the dirt sent up helpless blessings,

disguises for the escape route
I hoped never to need.
The flowers were spectacular when I left.

Now I hold the lost house like a book before me,
heavy as granite on weak knees.
The habit of close reading,

like some of the habits of love,
is hard to let go.
Because I learned so much from it,

I came to think I was nothing without words.
Even the borrowed ones
fell sweetly on my ear,

echoes of unanswerable questions—
"Why didn't you love me?"—
that come back as *love me,*

words of one syllable
rising up into the air,
thick with tardy wings.

White Twilight

A ghost gets up
and hurries, sick,
to the bathroom.
I can hear him
getting rid of his bad habits.
But he's long gone,
not even the smell left
in the white twilight.
No, it is morning.
Bathroom clean and steaming.
White light behind curtains
like new canvases,
screens, manuscripts.
Like health,
if I could believe it,
beginning, not ending,
not white twilight
like a long bleached sheet
laid down for the bride
to tread on,
path into the fog.

Shepherd on the Rocks, with a Twist

Deep in my ancestral cells
a little Scotsman is hopping up and down
clutching his dirk.
Old MacDonald, hot for vengeance,
wakes me up at night with a dose of iron shavings
to thrill my blood.

How to stay sane in grief and anger:
make up fantasies,
believe you weren't Hitler, not even a bad guy—
nobody's bad anymore, just wrong, just hungry.
Hoot mon! You weren't Hitler!
The dirk falls from my teeth like a rose
and cuts my toe.
Bring on the sheep stomach and the single malt.

> We traveled in ice-cold Cornwall.
> Improbable lianas in Barbara Hepworth's
> studio garden,
> burnt traces of her tragic death removed
> for the supremacy of art's fruited limbs.

> You snapped me in a puffy coat,
> eager to take my arm, to watch the sea
> display itself,
> sculpting and re-sculpting its surface,
> beating up against the land-spit.

> Frigid air drew us together
> until we grew accustomed to the strangeness.
> A kind of warmth,
> like the blue and yellow ribbons of a fake fire.

After the mask is—the mask.
Look here, where the line is.
Blake would say the universe begins there,
a huge blue-black space
one sculpts into gardens, houses, boats,
then sets them on fire to recover the loneliness
of an old scowling shepherd, eyes glaring
above his ratty beard.
Old Pictish Mac, brazenly unforgiving.
I love the sound of his hoots and howls.

The end's not in sight. It's still winter.
Branches are laden and dangerous.
Confused birds try to land, take off
on cold feet. Animals watch their breath
gather around their faces in steamy clouds,
grateful not to be thinking
though they know grief.
Absence in the fall of darkness
that brings no key.

> I went a little way along the ice-path
> you had not shoveled, and fell.
> All morning anger had hot-wired the house,
> the furnace blared and kept clearing its throat.
> After the freeze and thaw, a flood.
> I held up the arm-cast while pulling
> the garden-hose for our neighbor Bill
> to hook to the sump pump.
>
> Later, dreaming of her, you embraced me.
> What's that funny smell?

>Pills, booze, funky perfume?
>Some of these pills can make you psychotic.

>Officer, I didn't know.
>The head came off right in my hands.
>It was still muttering.

After the mask is the mask.
Invisible stitches, a comfortable fit,
jokes, smiles, spectacular dinners.
Glenmorangie, golden-amber
above the grins of the guests.
A real fire tumbles over itself,
anxious to please.

The new season seems to repeat last year
but unidentifiable forms
of ice gather on tree limbs
ready at last to go. Deep in the night
large branches whump into the drifts
and I don't hear or see.

>You think I am at the end of this?
>You think there's an end?

Time to take off the kilt now
and fold it into a drawer. In a few hours
it'll stop jigging. The slow little plane
banks steeply over green cliffs and sheep fields.
Lonely men look up. Then I come
to two people shouting on opposite crags,
Love me! Love ME!
deaf to each other.
The plane gathers speed,
it wants to rise above it all.
The engine is so quiet
you would think it had died,

but it keeps going, looking for a place
to swim between the clouds.
In a few hours it will be somewhere else,
tired from its brief accomplishment,
the momentary journey above memory's
last arresting sight—
the hungry sheep look up and are not fed.

A Woman Holding a Balance

I have let in just enough light
to show my eyes what my hands do.
It falls on coins, on pearls,
a ray that reaches into the deep
where a laden wreck rocks.
On these things that have come to nothing
I let my sight abide
and pick up the scales,
weighing the little I ask for
with the little I get.
When the sun comes up strong,
busy with query and preparedness,
the scales will tilt and chatter
with the work of the world.
Waiting is the portion I measure,
to sort the indifference and the rage
from the secret joy.

Jane Austen in January

The plough-man won't show
   so it's just Jane and me
in the weary snowlight.
   Caught in her net,
I move into a world so small
   its heroine has never seen the sea.
Is disappearance, I wonder,
   the same as hiding—
a film over the eyes, then a veil,
   then a drift of white mica,
the character trapped inside,
   guilty and crying,
thinned to a few lines on paper.
   How much the branches can bear
the next few hours will tell,
   a small lesson
held inside the course of a day.
   I want to be inside the snow,
inside a book where learning is safe,
   even on the head of a pin,
but behind the screen of trees
   is the shadow of someone
I must never love again, if he exists.
   The shadow of the *if*
is the ice on the footpath
   I'll clear when I'm ready,
alone, witless, hoping against hope.

The Death of the Fall

When the cornfields suddenly burnish
and one red branch
among green maple leaves waves its flag,
I know I am at the edge where language
sees what it cannot do.
Passing through, or passed through,
I am the whole sentence I speak,
each word, even the least ones,
alive as birds. I hear their songs disintegrate,
regroup at a colder command
received from the arrangement of stars.
My neighbor with his barrow,
emerging from the laden, gold-green field,
is as tired as work can make a man,
and beyond talk. That's how he knows he lives,
must live, as long as his seed lasts.

The Shape

I carry a shape,
warm from breastbone
down to tucked-in
legs, curled against me
asleep, the cat
against my body.

I carry it always,
this visible
missing one
like a degree of fever
wrapped in a chill,
waking in the night,
as sleep shifts
to gray nights, gone.

You can read me
by this shape,
the way you name
the soul of someone
in a face long flown away,
a name forgotten,
carried about
in quickening air.

Algebra

"Take X." His huge hand sketched.
"Where does it come from, the air?"
I squinted. The air loosened,
a raggedy X came out and perched
in the charged space between our fingers.

Sadness sat in his eyes,
warm white around trembling irises;
the long wide mouth played at a smile.
Around us, a lot full of fat cars
ready for people with packages.
Who'd sit still for math?
Not this ninth-grade granddaughter
with a restless, experimental face.

His neck rose straight up from his spine,
columnar, stark as a chimney
in its rust of fires.
An old house, an old patient place,
witness, watcher . . . .
Take a white slow summer cloud,
last breath of his small brother
the stove caught. Take X.

Across the equal sign
he calls from his home in space.
Still he reads the fair field of my voice.

Second Glance

The desiccated bird was just a leaf
until I looked again and saw a bird.
A grief requires a mind to be a grief.

Seizing on words too early for relief,
language makes a law of the absurd.
The desiccated bird was just a leaf,

as senseless as a mockingbird gone deaf
and mute for plagiarizing what it heard.
A grief demands a mind to be a grief

whose second glance, belief or disbelief,
discloses what denial has obscured—
the desiccated bird is not a leaf,

although its ground-time here will be as brief
as comfort lasts, delivered in a word.
A grief appropriates a mind with grief.

Of all the forms of mindlessness, the chief
is saying what occurred has not occurred.
The fallen bird has withered like a leaf.
A grief arranges minds within its grief.

Distance

In a few days you will marry again.
I was your second wife. We are not friends.
I'm making this as short as I possibly can
but something must be said. That is the law
of the life of words, a law that must be kept
and broken at once, in the way footprints
describe the road forward, the road back.
Clouds bank against the noonday empty sky,
beyond them, stars invisible as years,
whose names we use for distance, even as silence
is the hollow between unspoken waves.

Another Life

"That was in another life," we say.
Everyone knows what that means—
another love, another country.
"In another life, when I drank chartreuse,
densely herbal, fresh green on my tongue,
the light filtering through new rainwater
fell on a face beside a café window . . . ."
I hear about another's other life
which seems happier than the other lives
I've led—how could I have been
the one that led those other lives?
A few sprigs of green at Christmastime,
no tree. I'd put lights on the schefflera,
open some wine, secretly listen to the Festival
of Lessons and Carols on the radio,
in another life dreaming of another life.
Now I am in the life I dreamed of,
or am I? The borders of the world
are still lit with gold, uncertain radiance,
shimmering beyond the wing of an airplane
or over the lip of a glass. Someone's other life
flickers in his eyes, still beautiful,
closed off, complete. When he looks up
he looks at me as if I were a stranger
looking at him as if he were a stranger.

The Undertow

The Undertow

Today is my fiftieth birthday.
I wanted her here for the party, bringing
her recipe for hot crab dip,
her lusters of colors and flowers,
her jokes about weird guests. I wanted
my friends to clasp her hands
and say how alike we are.
But when I hold out my hand to clear
the cloud from her mirror,
there's her engagement ring,
the mysterious cleaved surface
deepening its shine
on my knobby, unpolished finger.
A woman can get used to anything,
she said, even diamonds,
but what will I be when I am past
the big waves, forgetful, even happy
in the clean dappled shadows?

The night she died, the young nurse
complained she couldn't budge the ring off,
news that kept me bad company
on the flight south through thunderheads.
I stared out the window. Would I see her
on her sudden flight upward?
The heaven Daddy saw
lay all around me
like a harbor of foggy ships.

A gleam far below
signaled a plane gradually climbing north,
its wingtip a small solitaire
rescued from the ashes.

Some fool mail that arrived
ten days after his death
said, "Now that you're single . . ." She hooted,
"I sent it back with 'You can kiss my butt'."
Our last talk was of shopping,
her sport, her art.
She was a heat-seeking missile
in the vast malls of Atlanta,
planning her widowhood
in a series of nice outfits
to keep out the cold.
She admired the black Talbot's bargain
I bought in ten minutes,
a dress to help me
step from phrase to phrase of my eulogy
like the CEO of Eulogies, Inc.,
maven of the tiny sandwich, the silver platter,
the fresh gobbets and guzzles of comfort
swirling through gossip, memorious jazz.

At the second reception, I'm telling her,
in a little out-of-body gossip,
a neighbor was heard to comment,
"Now they've got their wings,"
as funny-horrible as a fly riding the lime
in my uncle's forbidden second highball.
Declining the pink gift jello
studded with fetal marshmallows,
my uncle retrieves a tale
about some neighborhood boy in Copper Hill
who found him a live horse to ride on
to impress that cute slim with green eyes

living in the skimpy little house,
the kind of orphan people fall for,
who just knows she's got royal blood
but won't say so. Anyhow, this boy
fell right off the steed at her feet;
I can see her trying not to laugh,
but blushing at this proof
that things in books really do happen
even in a red-dirt holler in the hills.

Everything's under control, the plot paid for,
the dresses steamed, the hair done;
isn't this better than wondering
if he's going to set fire to the house when left alone,
or how many riffs of Basie and Goodman
it'll take to raise a smile
on his thin mottled cheeks?
But dying takes as long as it needs.
Close to shore, the wind drops, the sails hang
chalk-dry against the masts.
Across the huge water our whispers, our tears,
our stupid jokes rattle like saucepan lids,
birds flap among the beetles and disappear.

On the preacher's second visit
he charms her, she charms him
(he has an eye for the ladies).
None of us knows that in a month
he'll be reading Proverbs at her service,
that bit about a good woman
whose price is far above rubies.
The scripture lays a jeweled lid
over the tiny box of bone and ash
next to my father's fresh square
not far from the park bench they sat on
in the wistful September night
after the war had just begun,

when he asked her to wait for him,
and, being a good woman, she said yes,
and, being a good woman, didn't think much
about the cost of goodness.

After the false alarm, when the throat,
the testicle, the duodenum, the hip,
the kidney, the kidney, poor prunes,
gave way and came back and gave way,
he lay on his back staring
at the trailing nightrobe of his mother

the way Moses looked upon
God's shadowy back.
We watched the weather of confusion
clear from his face as the minor devils
scuttled back into the chemicals that birthed them—
the imp whirling around on the fan
laughing, the sullen cloud of flies
from the curtains.
Then clean light beckoned in the doorway.

My brother and I wake up.
At three-thirty she comes in.
Her voice is high with disbelief,
she's full of apology as if the flood
has risen to the window and the boat is waiting
to bundle in the sleepy kids and the cat.
He's cold to the touch, and hard,
sealed off, like nothing I've ever felt,
his temple a metal plate over the winked-out lights.
When she says, "Goodbye, my love,"
I know that he held it all for her, a life
beyond the reach of illness or coldness
or the scuffed footprints on the roads
that led them nowhere.

She'd kill me for telling this,
even though she knew no censor
and mixed the sweets with the spoils.
Up north it's different.
Scared of the twang of girlhood,
I cling to the skimpy handrails
lest I dive straight toward the blind albino fish
way down deep in Mammoth,
freaks of nature pale from adaptation
to a dead-end world.

     At my back
the sour-breath Presbyterian God
who's no God at all but a company
called The Institutes written by a constipated
gray-faced buzzard in Geneva,
gets his claws in my neck. "Look here,"
he says, "*Of course, absolutely*
these deaths are a law you can't change,
but you must figure it out
as if you invented it." John Calvin,
you can kiss my butt. She's not where
you think, and just for that
I'm repapering heaven in the colors she liked,
celadon green and wine, and giving him back
the toys you took away when you scared him
into absolute goodness: the drum brushes,
the Artie Shaw records, the tennis racket,
and finally the golf clubs, not to mention
the murder books and bar gizmos
with which he'd mix Rob Roys and Presbyterians
and for all I know, John Knoxes
for their friends on hot summer nights.

Of course this poem's my banjo, my Dobro,
my twelve-string Gibson I'm playing

to chime in with my brother's mandolin
as our voices rise up in the ancient
hillbilly lament, *whaunnnh,* part curse,
part yodel, that comes out of me
past years of book-larnin'
and says you can take all of it in
and dress up with it, climb up to a pulpit
to read a poem like a good daughter
and then something else has to happen,
the big black birds have to gather in the garden
to mock what you made, and this is the sound
you make to mock them back.

She and I are going through my closet.
"I wish you could wear my shoes,"
she says, and I tell her where they've gone,
Viet Nam Vets, battered women,
Goodwill. She's reading my mind again:
"Don't wear that black dress. Not for a birthday.
Not even with a diamond on your finger."
OK, I won't. I'll pretend
it came to me in a dream; that it all
came in a dream, that soon some hurricane
from the Azores will spin up here
and gather up the oak chest, the cinnabar vases,
the needlepoint footstool, the diamond,
whirl them back to Georgia and set them down
just where they ought to be,
the chair with her glasses on it; his chair
with the warmed-up cat, the gas fire
pretending to nibble at the cinders.

I know that her next sentence,
beginning with "Remember,"
will work the knot of a miracle.
Sure enough, we're back on the beach,

or rather in the water, way out,
on a rubber raft. The sun washes us,
the salt water burns, she looks up, slips off the side
and with urgent strokes keeps pulling
against the current. I can see the muscles
in her neck and arms, so I'm not crying
even though we're in danger. The water, the sun
feel so good I can accept anything they do,
and any force that pulls me, that pulls her,
as long as we're moving together,
is a furrow she ploughs in time
while I move easily behind, scattering drops
of water from my hair like seeds,
one for each year of the life
she gave back to me.

PHOTO BY PETER CZAP

SUSAN SNIVELY grew up in Louisville, Kentucky, and now lives in New England, where she is the director of the Writing Center at Amherst College. She teaches courses in writing and autobiographies of women, and has published two collections of poems, *From This Distance* (1981) and *Voices in the House* (1988). She has recently finished the manuscript of her first novel, *The Power to Kill*.

University of Central Florida
Contemporary Poetry Series

Diane Averill, *Branches Doubled Over with Fruit*
Jennifer Bates, *The First Night Out of Eden*
George Bogin, *In a Surf of Strangers*
Van K. Brock, *The Hard Essential Landscape*
Jean Burden, *Taking Light from Each Other*
Lynn Butler, *Planting the Voice*
Cathleen Calbert, *Lessons in Space*
Daryl Ngee Chinn, *Soft Parts of the Back*
Robert Cooperman, *In the Household of Percy Bysshe Shelley*
Rebecca McClanahan Devet, *Mother Tongue*
Rebecca McClanahan Devet, *Mrs. Houdini*
Gerald Duff, *Calling Collect*
Malcolm Glass, *Bone Love*
Barbara L. Greenberg, *The Never-Not Sonnets*
Susan Hartman, *Dumb Show*
Lola Haskins, *Forty-four Ambitions for the Piano*
Lola Haskins, *Planting the Children*
William Hathaway, *Churlsgrace*
William Hathaway, *Looking into the Heart of Light*
Michael Hettich, *A Small Boat*
Ted Hirschfield, *Middle Mississippians: Encounters with the Prehistoric Amerindians*
Roald Hoffmann, *Gaps and Verges*
Roald Hoffmann, *The Metamict State*
Greg Johnson, *Aid and Comfort*
Markham Johnson, *Collecting the Light*
Hannah Kahn, *Time, Wait*
Michael McFee, *Plain Air*
Richard Michelson, *Tap Dancing for the Relatives*
Judith Minty, *Dancing the Fault*
David Posner, *The Sandpipers*
Nicholas Rinaldi, *We Have Lost Our Fathers*
CarolAnn Russell, *The Red Envelope*
Robert Siegel, *In a Pig's Eye*
Edmund Skellings, *Face Value*
Edmund Skellings, *Heart Attacks*
Floyd Skloot, *Music Appreciation*
Ron Smith, *Running Again in Hollywood Cemetery*
Susan Snively, *The Undertow*
Katherine Soniat, *Cracking Eggs*
Don Stap, *Letter at the End of Winter*
Rawdon Tomlinson, *Deep Red*
Irene Willis, *They Tell Me You Danced*
John Woods, Black Marigolds